Yolanda's All Apple Cookbook

Best Wishes —
Yolanda Lodi

Also by YOLANDA LODI

Yolanda's Cranberry Country Recipes

Yolanda's Hand-Me-Down Recipes

Yolanda's Blueberry Cookbook

Yolanda's All New Cranberry Cookbook

Yolanda's
All Apple Cookbook

YOLANDA LODI

ROCK VILLAGE
PUBLISHING

Middleborough, Massachusetts

ISBN 978-1-934400-21-0

Rock Village Publishing
41 Walnut Street
Middleborough MA 02346
(508) 946-4738
rockvillage@verizon.net

Dedication

TO THE FOLKS AT COUNTRY PRESS

IN APPRECIATION OF THEIR PROFESSIONALISM
AND OUTSTANDING SERVICE

Contents

Introduction

Breakfast & Brunch

Side Dishes

Poultry

Contents

Seafood

Cakes & Brownies

Buckle & Tortes

Pies

Crisps

Yolanda's
All Apple Cookbook

Introduction

A Peek at What's Inside

‧∽◌∽‧

The recipes in *Yolanda's All Apple Cookbook* are nutritious and easy to prepare. One of my favorites is Old-Fashioned Apple Pie, for a couple of reasons. When I was a child my father would sit at the kitchen table peeling apples from his own trees while my mother made pie crust from scratch. That fond memory became alive for me the day I made this pie from our own espaliered apple tree that my husband, Ed, and I bought more than fifteen years ago. I hardly dared hope that it would produce apples for a scrumptious apple pie. But it did!

Another favorite is Apple Walnut Crispy Crust Pie. "It's worth doing a cookbook for just this one recipe," says my husband. It's so easy. There is no crust to bother with; the batter over the top of the apple slices creates its own crispy crust.

If you're looking for an apple pie comparable to those bought in gourmet pastry shops, look no further than Delicious Pecan Pie. The Golden Delicious apples used in this recipe create an eye-appealing finished pie that will be sure to please.

Another dessert, other than pie, that is a work of art in baking is a torte. One that deserves special recognition is Agnes's Apple Torte. Although the recipe takes some time to make it's well worth the results, for not only the artistic arrangement of the apple slices standing on end, but also the rich taste in each mouthful. I can see why this recipe won first prize in "The Great Apple Cake Bake Off 2005." I would like to extend my many thanks to Agnes Munap, who is now 94 years old and still bakes all her favorite recipes, for sharing this recipe with me, and to her daughter-in-law, Janice Belasco, for taking the time to send it.

Another special winning recipe is Auntie's Apple Pudding Cake. Kathleen Sousa's favorite aunt gave her this recipe 30 years ago. She says, "Her apple pudding cake always warms my belly as thoughts of her warm my heart." Thank you for sharing an apple recipe that my family and friends enjoyed immensely.

While on the subject of cakes I cannot go any further without mentioning Dottie's Apple Cake. This is one great, old recipe that works with whatever types of apples you have on hand. I know! I used a combination of different apples and the outcome was a very moist and scrumptious cake. Dottie Dudley, thank you for sending your recipe and for taking the time to talk to me.

Having friends over for dinner and want to serve something that looks and smells enticing? How about Spicy Applesauce Cake? It not only smells delicious as it's baking in the oven but it continues to permeate the air with its spices as it sits on a plate waiting to be eaten. Let me share a little story with you. Last year I invited friends over for dinner. Amongst the appetizers I placed on the coffee table I included slices of this cake. Just before we sat down for dinner I looked over and noticed that all the slices of Spicy Applesauce Cake had vanished.

Ask me what my favorite treat is and I'm torn between Apple Fudge Cake and Apple Nut Brownies. Both are very moist with an intense chocolate flavor. Each mouthful tastes like a piece of fudge. The secret is to use high quality unsweetened cocoa powder, such as Ghirardelli (which can be bought at your local grocery store at a reasonable price). If push comes to shove I must confess that the Apple Nut Brownies would be my first choice for a couple of reasons. They're loaded with nuts, which I love, and they freeze very well, so I always have a treat waiting for me in the freezer. Anyone who knows me knows that I ration the sweets I eat and that I love chocolate. I always say, "You don't have to eat it all in one day."

Buckles are cake-like desserts made with fresh fruit; they usually contain berries. Not many are made with apples like my Apple Walnut Buckle. The baking apples used in this recipe make a moist, sweet-tasting dessert that resembles a buckle, especially with the diced apples peeking through the top.

I've included six crisp recipes, three of which contain either blueberries and/or cranberries along with apples. Every year I not only freeze fresh blueberries that my husband and I pick locally during the summer, but I also freeze fresh cranberries that I buy at the annual Cranberry Harvest Festival in Wareham, Massachusetts. Because of my love for these berries I developed Apple Berry Crisp. This recipe along with Apple Cranberry Crisp and Blueberry Apple Crisp are new to this cookbook. For those readers who collect cookbooks you will not find them in my previous cookbooks, *Yolanda's Blueberry Cookbook* and *Yolanda's All New Cranberry Cookbook*.

Before I go any further I need to tell you where I got the idea for this cookbook. A couple of years ago (not too long after my *All New Cranberry Cookbook* was published) my good friend Carolyn Gilmore surprised me with a bag containing several varieties of local apples, some perfect for eating, others with marks and bruises that needed to be used up soon. What better way than in a crisp? First came Apple Oatmeal Crisp, and then the above mentioned recipes.

While I was working on this cookbook Maureen Dion sent me My Pen Pal's Apple Crisp. She wrote, "This apple crisp is the best I've ever had thanks to a pen pal who always exchanges recipes with me." She's absolutely right. Besides the ten to twelve apples (I used twelve), the recipe also has you pouring three-quarters of a cup of melted butter over the top. That's one and one-half sticks of butter; a little bit more than I would normally use, but it's what keeps the crisp moist and makes this a winning recipe.

"This recipe passes the taste test of my three grown boys so I know it's a winner," writes Anne Carey. Anne's Squash with Apples Casserole is definitely a winner, whether you use fresh apples, which I prefer, or canned apples, as Anne does at times when she doesn't have fresh apples on hand. What better way to serve butternut squash?

Since one of my favorite vegetables, especially in the fall, is butternut squash, I tried combining it with two popular fruits, apples and cranberries, that are readily available this time of year. The result was a delicious recipe called Apple Boats.

Don't sail away till you read about my Apple Awesome, included in the "side dishes" section of this cookbook. I like this recipe so much that I've thought of warming up the leftovers and serving it as a dessert with a dollop of whipped cream; definitely not a dessert for those who are only satisfied with a sweet ending to their meal.

Whipped cream or ice cream? Which will it be this year to top off Ms. Boudreau's Applesauce? Jennifer Boudreau teaches kindergarten and makes this recipe each year with her students.

A scoop of ice cream on top of a slice of Apple Pecan Bread sounds good to me. This bread is so moist that you could serve it as a cake. A couple of other breads deserve to be mentioned. For a scrumptiously delicious treat, toast a one-inch slice of Nutty Apple Bread and spread on a little bit of butter. I bet you can't eat just one slice. Apple Parmesan Bread makes a nice addition to a special dinner. The shiny, crusty outer shell of this bread, along with the not-too sweet taste, goes great with any meal, whether it's chicken or seafood.

Just a couple of months ago I served the Apple Parmesan Bread with Baked Stuffed Shrimp. This recipe stuffs 16 to 20 shrimp, depending upon the size of the jumbo tail-on shrimp. The apples and Parmesan in both recipes complement each other. The same holds true for Chicken Delicious. In this recipe the red pepper gives a colorful presentation. Every bite is so moist with a unique hint of sweetness that you don't even realize that fruit and vegetables were used in the preparation. The same holds true for some of the other entrées, such as Apple Walnut Chicken Salad and Apple Turkey Loaf.

There are some side dishes for vegetarians to consider as lunch entrées. (Just double up on the portions.) These include Vegetable Wild Rice with Apple Bits and Apple-Spiced Bulgar, a recipe offering many health benefits from the grain, fruits, and vegetables. Another dish that can be served as an entrée for lunch with a salad, but which I've included in the "breakfast and brunch" section, is Apple-Veggie Omelette. The combination of vegetables, apple, and cheese makes this a tasty, satisfying dish. Surprise your family with this recipe or maybe with the next one, especially in the fall.

Celebrate fall with fresh cranberries and Macoun apples with dumplings for breakfast, Apple Cranberry Oven-Baked Dumplings. Macoun apples are tree ripened (not like some of the shipped apples you buy in the stores) and are only available locally in the fall. I discovered them while I was putting this cookbook together. Looking for a large quantity of baking apples I stopped by a farm stand in Acushnet, Massachusetts, owned by Ernie and Diane Ventura. Their sign reads Ashley's Peaches, but I soon learned that they also grow and sell Macoun apples. After spending some time talking with Ernie, who explained that these apples don't last long and cannot be stored for the winter, and that the baked goods on the table were made by his wife using Macouns, I bought a big bag. For many of the recipes that state baking apples I used the apples I bought that day. I'm looking forward to returning next fall and maybe, meeting and talking to Mrs. Ventura.

One of the recipes for which I used the Macoun apples is Marilyn's Fresh Apple Squares. "Everyone looks forward to my apple squares at the coffee hour that follows our Fellowship Meeting at my church," was Marilyn Legge's comment to me when I called to let her know that I would be including her recipe in my book. It is refreshing to see someone using fresh fruit in squares instead of canned fruit. It surely makes a difference.

Coffee hour reminds me of Apple Raisin Coffeecake. This moist, not too sweet coffeecake takes no time to prepare and smells wonderful as it bakes. It's a great cake for breakfast or brunch.

Since I started this introduction with pies I thought I would end it with a recipe for Apple-Nut Breakfast Pie. Don't be fooled. This looks like a puffy pie, but has the texture of bread pudding without the extra calories contained in some bread pudding recipes. You can also use it as a dessert; just add a scoop of vanilla ice cream.

If you just finished reading this short introduction, you probably realize that I'm having fun sharing these recipes. I love to cook as I'm sure you do, too. My goal in writing this book is to encourage you to take chances in experimenting with different ingredients. Try something new that sounds good. Start with fresh ingredients that you're familiar with and then experiment. Write the recipe, or better still, type it up on your computer and print a hard copy. As you're making the recipe make the necessary adjustments and jot them down. You don't want to leave that perfect recipe to memory. Before you know it you will have created your own cookbook to share with family and friends! If you need help give me a call or send me an e-mail. I may not have the answer, but I'm sure we'll enjoy talking about recipes.

Have fun! And keep cooking!

Yolanda Lodi
Middleborough, Massachusetts

Breakfast & Brunch

Breakfast & Brunch

Apple Raisin Coffeecake

 ¼ cup (½ stick) butter, softened
 ¾ cup sugar
 1 large egg
 ½ cup skim milk
1½ cups all-purpose flour
 2 tsp. baking powder
 ¼ tsp. salt
 ½ cup raisins
 2 medium apples, peeled, cored, and sliced

Topping

 2 Tbsp. sugar
 2 Tbsp. all-purpose flour
 1 Tbsp. chilled butter, cut into small pieces
 ☙ Ground cinnamon (to sprinkle over top)
 ☙ Sugar (to sprinkle over top)

*This moist, not too sweet, coffeecake takes
no time to prepare and smells wonderful
as it bakes in the oven.*

Breakfast & Brunch

Preheat oven to 350 degrees.

Grease and flour a 9-inch square baking pan.

In a large bowl, with mixer at low speed, cream butter and sugar until smooth and fluffy. Add egg. Beat until well blended.

Stir in milk until combined.

Add flour, baking powder, and salt. Mix with a spoon until the dry ingredients are moistened.

Fold in raisins.

Using a spatula spread batter into greased and floured pan.

Arrange apple slices evenly on top of the batter.

Topping

In a small bowl mix sugar and flour. Using a pastry cutter cut in butter until mixture forms crumbs.

Sprinkle over apple slices. Then sprinkle cinnamon and sugar.

Bake at 350 degrees for 40 minutes or until toothpick inserted in center comes out clean.

Makes 9 servings.

Breakfast & Brunch

Marilyn's Fresh Apple Squares

- 2 cups all-purpose flour
- 1 cup sugar
- ½ cup (1 stick) butter
- 1 cup pecan pieces
- 2 tsp. ground cinnamon
- 1 tsp. baking soda
- ½ tsp. salt
- 1 large egg
- 1 cup sour cream
- 1 tsp. vanilla extract
- 2 cups apples, peeled, cored, and finely chopped

*"Everyone looks forward to my apple squares
at the coffee hour that follows our Fellowship Meeting
at my church."* – MARILYN LEGGE

4

Breakfast & Brunch

Preheat oven to 350 degrees.

In a large bowl combine flour and sugar. Using a pastry cutter, cut in butter until crumbly. Stir in pecan pieces.

Press ¾ cup of crumbly mixture into an ungreased 13- x 9- x 2-inch baking pan.

To the remaining crumbly mixture add cinnamon, baking soda, salt, egg, sour cream, and vanilla extract. Blend well. (Batter will be stiff.)

Stir in chopped apples.

Spoon batter evenly over pressed crumbs in baking pan.

Bake at 350 degrees for 30 to 40 minutes.

Cool on a wire rack.

Cut into squares.

Serve with whipped cream or sprinkle with powdered sugar.

Makes 12 to 16 servings.

Breakfast & Brunch

Apple-Nut Breakfast Pie

3   Tbsp. butter
2   medium Granny Smith apples, peeled, cored, and thinly sliced
$^1/_2$ cup chopped walnuts

Pancake Batter

4   large eggs
1   cup skim milk
$^2/_3$ cup all-purpose flour
2   Tbsp. sugar
1   tsp. vanilla extract
$^1/_2$ tsp. ground cinnamon
   Confectioners' sugar (to sprinkle over top after baking)

This looks like a puffy pie, but has the texture of bread pudding without the extra calories contained in some bread pudding recipes.

Breakfast & Brunch

Preheat oven to 425 degrees.

Generously butter the bottom and sides of a deep dish 9.5-inch glass pie plate.

In a medium saucepan melt butter over medium heat. Add apple slices. Cook over medium-high heat, stirring constantly with a wooden spoon, until apples are tender.

Arrange cooked apple slices evenly on bottom of pie plate. Sprinkle chopped walnuts over top of apples. Set aside.

Pancake Batter

In a large bowl beat eggs until foamy. Add milk, flour, sugar, vanilla extract, and cinnamon. Beat until well blended.

Pour batter over the walnut covered apple slices.

Bake at 425 degrees for 23 to 25 minutes or until knife inserted in center comes out clean and top is puffy and golden brown.

Serve immediately with a generous sprinkle of confectioners' sugar.

Makes 4 servings.

Breakfast & Brunch

Apple Parmesan Bread

¹/₂ cup (1 stick) butter, melted

³/₄ cup sugar

2 large eggs

2¹/₂ cups all-purpose flour

1 tsp. baking powder

1 tsp. baking soda

¹/₄ tsp. salt

1 medium apple, peeled, cored, and finely diced

¹/₂ cup Parmesan, finely shredded cheese

¹/₄ cup chopped walnuts

*The shiny, crusty outer shell of this bread,
along with the not-too sweet taste, makes each slice
a nice addition to a special dinner.*

Breakfast & Brunch

Preheat oven to 350 degrees.

Grease and flour a 9- x 5- x 3-inch loaf pan.

In a large bowl, with mixer at low speed, cream butter and sugar until light and fluffy. Add one egg at a time, making sure batter continues to be fluffy.

In a separate bowl sift together flour, baking powder, baking soda, and salt.

Add sifted, dry ingredients to creamed mixture, alternately with diced apples, blending well after each addition.

Add shredded Parmesan cheese and stir. (Batter will be stiff.)

Fold in chopped walnuts.

Pour batter into greased and floured loaf pan.

Bake at 350 degrees for 50 to 55 minutes or until toothpick inserted in center comes out clean.

Cool on a wire rack.

Makes 1 loaf.

Breakfast & Brunch

Apple Pecan Bread

2 large eggs

1 cup sugar

½ cup vegetable oil

2 Tbsp. vanilla yogurt

½ tsp. vanilla extract

2 cups all-purpose flour

1 tsp. baking soda

1 tsp. ground cinnamon

½ tsp. salt

1 cup apples, peeled, cored, and chopped

½ cup pecans, finely diced

*This bread is so moist that you can serve
it as a cake with a scoop of ice cream.*

Breakfast & Brunch

Preheat oven to 350 degrees.

Grease and flour a 9- x 5- x 3-inch loaf pan.

In a large bowl, with mixer at low speed, combine eggs and sugar. Add oil, yogurt, and vanilla extract. Beat well.

In a separate bowl sift together flour, baking soda, cinnamon, and salt.

Add dry ingredients to large bowl, stirring with a spoon, until the dry ingredients are moistened.

Fold in chopped apples and diced pecans.

Pour batter into greased and floured baking pan.

Bake at 350 degrees for 55 to 60 minutes or until toothpick inserted in center comes out clean.

Cool on a wire rack.

Makes 1 loaf.

Breakfast & Brunch

Nutty Apple Bread

½ cup (1 stick) butter, softened
1 cup sugar
2 large eggs
1 medium tart apple, peeled and grated
2 cups all-purpose flour
1 tsp. baking powder
1 tsp. baking soda
⅛ tsp. salt
½ cup walnuts, finely diced

For a scrumptiously delicious breakfast treat,
toast a one-inch slice of this bread and
spread on a little bit of butter.
I bet you can't eat just one slice.

Breakfast & Brunch

Preheat oven to 350 degrees.

Grease and flour a 9- x 5- x 3-inch loaf pan.

In a large bowl, with mixer at low speed, cream butter and sugar until smooth and fluffy. Add one egg at a time, making sure batter continues to be fluffy.

Stir in grated apple.

In a separate bowl sift together flour, baking powder, baking soda, and salt.

Add sifted ingredients to large bowl. Mix with a spoon until the dry ingredients are moistened. (Batter will be stiff.)

Fold in finely diced walnuts.

Pour batter into greased and floured loaf pan. Using a spatula spread batter evenly into the corners.

Bake at 350 degrees for 45 minutes.

Cover with aluminum foil.

Bake for an **additional** 10 minutes or until toothpick inserted in center comes out clean.

Cool on a wire rack.

Makes 1 loaf.

Apple Walnut Muffins

  2   cups all-purpose flour
 1/3 cup sugar
  1   Tbsp. baking powder
 1/2 tsp. ground cinnamon
 1/4 tsp. salt
  1   large egg
  1   cup skim milk
  3   Tbsp. butter, melted
  1   small tart apple, peeled and grated
 1/2 cup walnuts, finely diced

Maybe I should call these muffins "biscuits."
The crunchy outer shell with a soft bread-like
center offers a special treat when added to a bread basket.

Breakfast & Brunch

Preheat oven to 400 degrees.

Grease twelve-2½-inch-muffin-cup pan well with butter.

In a large bowl combine flour, sugar, baking powder, cinnamon, and salt.

In a medium-sized bowl whisk egg. Add milk and melted butter. Whisk until foamy. Stir in grated apple.

Add apple-egg mixture to the large bowl. Stir with a spoon until the dry ingredients are moistened.

Fold in **half** (¼ cup) finely diced walnuts.

Spoon batter into muffin pan.

Sprinkle remaining walnuts over top of batter.

Bake at 400 degrees for 22 to 25 minutes or until toothpick inserted in center comes out clean.

Makes 12 muffins.

Breakfast & Brunch

Tasty Corn Muffins

1   cup all-purpose flour
3/4   cup yellow cornmeal
1/4   cup sugar
2   tsp. baking powder
1/2   tsp. baking soda
1/2   tsp. salt
1   cup sour cream
1   large egg
1/2   cup skim milk
2   Tbsp. butter, melted
1   medium apple, peeled and grated

*Corn muffins can sometimes be dry and crumbly,
but not these tasty ones. Their moist texture with
an added hint of apple will please even the fussiest guest.*

Breakfast & Brunch

Preheat oven to 375 degrees.

Grease twelve-2½-inch-muffin-cup pan well with butter.

In a large bowl combine flour, cornmeal, sugar, baking powder, baking soda, and salt.

Add sour cream, egg, milk, melted butter, and grated apple.

Stir with a spoon until the dry ingredients are moistened.

Spoon batter into muffin pan.

Bake at 375 degrees for 15 to 20 minutes or until toothpick inserted in center comes out clean.

Makes 12 muffins.

Breakfast & Brunch

Apple-Veggie Omelette

2 Tbsp. extra-virgin olive oil
1 medium onion, chopped
1 medium red pepper, chopped
2 garlic cloves, minced
1 medium apple, peeled, cored, and thinly sliced
4 large eggs
2 Tbsp. water
$^1\!/_2$ tsp. thyme leaves
$^1\!/_4$ tsp. ground nutmeg
$^1\!/_8$ tsp. ground black pepper
1 cup Parmesan, finely shredded cheese

*The combination of vegetables, apple, and cheese
makes this omelette a tasty, satisfying dish,
whether you serve it for breakfast or as an entrée
for lunch with a salad or side dish.*

Breakfast & Brunch

In a large skillet heat olive oil. Add onion, pepper, and garlic. Sauté until soft, but not browned.

Add apple slices. Cook over low heat, stirring occasionally with a wooden spoon, until apples are tender.

In a large bowl beat eggs, water, thyme, nutmeg, and black pepper until foamy. Pour this mixture over the apple-veggie mixture. Using a wooden spoon spread mixture evenly to sides of pan.

Sprinkle finely shredded Parmesan cheese over the top. Cover skillet.

Cook on low heat for 10 minutes or until eggs are set and cheese has melted.

Serve immediately.

Makes 4 servings.

Breakfast & Brunch

Apple Cranberry Oven-Baked Dumplings

4   medium Macoun apples, peeled, cored, and sliced
2   cups fresh cranberries, cut in half
½   cup sugar
½   tsp. ground cinnamon
½   tsp. ground ginger
¼   tsp. ground cloves

Dough

1   cup all-purpose flour
2   Tbsp. sugar
½   Tbsp. baking powder
3   Tbsp. chilled butter, cut into small pieces
½   cup skim milk
2   tsp. vanilla extract

*Celebrate fall with fresh cranberries and Macoun
apples by surprising your family
with dumplings for breakfast or as a snack!*

Preheat oven to 400 degrees.

Butter the bottom and sides of a 13- x 9- x 2-inch glass oven-proof baking dish.

Place apple slices on the bottom of a large saucepan. Then add cut cranberries. Sprinkle sugar and spices over the top.

Cover the pan and cook over low heat for 5 minutes.

Remove cover and stir with a wooden spoon until combined.

Cover the pan and increase heat to medium. Cook for an **additional** 5 to 7 minutes or until apples are tender.

Pour the apple/cranberry mixture into the buttered dish. Set aside.

Dough

In a large bowl sift together flour, sugar, and baking powder.

Using a pastry cutter, cut in butter until mixture forms crumbs.

Add milk and vanilla extract. Stir until the dry ingredients are moistened.

Spoon dough in dollops over top of apple/cranberry mixture.

Bake at 400 degrees for 20 to 25 minutes or until golden brown.

Serve warm with whipped cream.

Makes 8 servings.

Side Dishes

Side Dishes

Anne's Squash with Apples Casserole

5	lbs. butternut squash, peeled, seeded, and cubed
6	cups water
1	cup light brown sugar
3	medium baking apples, peeled, cored, and thinly sliced or 1 can (22 oz.) sliced apples
1½	cups (3 sticks) butter
1	tsp. ground cinnamon

"This recipe passes the taste test of my three grown boys so I know it's a winner. Enjoy." – ANNE CAREY

It is definitely a winner, whether you use fresh apples, which I prefer, or canned apples, as Anne does at times when she doesn't have fresh apples on hand.

Side Dishes

In a large pan cook cubed squash in water until tender.

Preheat oven to 350 degrees.

Drain well cooked squash in a colander. Use a potato masher to press any additional water through the colander.

Transfer cooked squash to a large bowl. Add sugar, apple slices, butter, and cinnamon.

Using a hand mixer mix together until all butter is melted. (The heat from the cooked squash will melt the butter.)

Pour mixture into a 13- x 9- x 2-inch glass oven-proof baking dish.

Bake at 350 degrees for 30 minutes or until bubbly.

Makes 8 to 10 servings.

Side Dishes

Apple Boats

1½ lbs. butternut squash, cut in half lengthwise and seeds removed
1   Tbsp. butter
2   small tart apples, peeled, cored, and chopped
1   cup cranberries, fresh or frozen, cut in half
½   Tbsp. dark-brown sugar
1   tsp. ground cinnamon
1   Tbsp. butter, cut into small pieces (to dot over top)
½   Tbsp. dark-brown sugar (to sprinkle over top)

Since one of my favorite vegetables, especially in the fall, is butternut squash, I tried combining it with two popular fruits, apples and cranberries, that are readily available this time of year. The result was this delicious recipe.

Side Dishes

Preheat oven to 375 degrees.

Lightly coat a glass oven-proof baking dish with olive oil.

Place squash cut-side up in baking dish and cover tightly with aluminum foil.

Bake at 375 degrees for 45 to 55 minutes or until squash is tender. (Do not overcook.)

While the squash is baking prepare filling:
In a medium saucepan melt butter over medium heat.

Add apples, cranberries, sugar, and cinnamon. Cook and stir over medium-high heat until apples are tender and cranberries pop.

Remove from stove. Set aside.

Allow cooked squash to cool slightly.

Scoop out most of the squash pulp (leave a one-half-inch-thick shell) into the saucepan containing the cooked filling.

Gently toss the cooked squash pieces with the fruit mixture.

Divide the filling in half and stuff each of the squash halves.

Dot with butter and sprinkle with sugar.

Bake uncovered at 350 degrees for about 20 to 25 minutes or until tops are crusty and brown.

Cool slightly before serving.

Makes 4 servings.

Side Dishes

Apple Port Sauce

7 medium cooking apples, peeled, cored, and coarsely chopped

½ cup Port wine

½ tsp. ground cinnamon

⅛ tsp. ground nutmeg

*This applesauce, which smells wonderful while cooking,
tastes perfectly sweet with no added sugar and is thick enough
to serve as an added treat with any festive dinner.
It's also great as a healthful snack.*

Side Dishes

Place all ingredients in a 2-quart saucepan.

On medium heat stir to boiling.

Reduce heat to simmer.

Stirring occasionally, cook for 5 to 10 minutes or until apples are tender.

Remove from heat.

Mash with a potato masher.

Stir and pour into a glass dish.

Ready to serve or refrigerate.

Makes about 2 cups.

Side Dishes

Ms. Boudreau's Applesauce

8 apples
$1/2$ cup water
$1/2$ cup brown sugar
$1/4$ tsp. ground cinnamon

"I teach kindergarten, and I make this recipe each year with my students. It is great with whipped cream or ice cream." – JENNIFER BOUDREAU

Side Dishes

Peel and core apples.

Cut apples into chunks.

Place apples, water, sugar, and cinnamon into a slow cooker.

Cook several hours until apples are mushy.

Cool and serve!

Makes 6 servings.

Side Dishes

Apple Awesome

5 medium baking apples, peeled, cored, and sliced
1 Tbsp. lemon juice
$1/2$ cup all-purpose flour
$1/2$ cup dark-brown sugar
$1/2$ tsp. ground cinnamon
$1/8$ tsp. salt
$1/4$ cup ($1/2$ stick) *cold* butter, cut into small pieces
1 cup shredded sharp Cheddar cheese

*Awesome is the only way I can describe this dish.
I like it so much that I've thought of warming up the leftovers
and serving it as a dessert with a dollop of whipped cream;
definitely not a dessert for those who are only satisfied
with a sweet ending to their meal.*

Side Dishes

Preheat oven to 350 degrees.

Butter the bottom and sides of an 8-inch square glass oven-proof baking dish.

Arrange apple slices in baking dish. Sprinkle with lemon juice.

In a large bowl whisk flour, sugar, cinnamon, and salt. Using a pastry cutter, cut in butter until mixture forms crumbs.

Stir in shredded cheese until combined.

Sprinkle crumbly mixture over top of apple slices.

Bake at 350 degrees for 35 to 40 minutes or until apples are tender.

Makes 6 servings.

Side Dishes

Apple Polenta

4	cups water
½	tsp. salt
1	cup yellow cornmeal
4	small tart apples, peeled, cored, and sliced

*"For breakfast my father would fry slabs of leftover polenta
until they became brown and crispy,"
said my husband as he placed the remaining polenta in the refrigerator.*

*The next morning I sliced the cold polenta, fried it up in butter,
and served it with coffee. Delicious! Reheated in the microwave
the following day, the fried slices tasted even better as a snack.*

Side Dishes

In a large pan bring water and salt to a full boil over medium-high heat.

Using a whisk to beat the cornmeal into the water, gradually sprinkle the cornmeal over the boiling water; reduce heat to medium when boiling becomes too intense and hot.

Continue to wisk vigorously to avoid lumps until all the cornmeal has been added to the pan.

Reduce heat to medium-low.

Continue whisking until mixture is smooth and small lumps no longer form.

Add apple slices. Cook, stirring constantly with a wooden spoon, until cornmeal thickens to the consistency of mashed potatoes and apples are tender *(about 20 minutes)*.

The polenta is ready when it comes easily away from the sides of the pan.

Remove from heat.

Let sit for 10 minutes.

Turn the polenta onto a warmed platter. Polenta can be scooped or sliced, depending how thick it is.

Makes 6 servings.

Side Dishes

Vegetable Wild Rice with Apple Bits

2   Tbsp. extra-virgin olive oil
1   cup celery, finely chopped
1   small onion, finely chopped
1   garlic clove, minced
³/₄ cup wild rice, rinsed and drained
1   can (14 oz.) vegetable broth, heated to hot
1   small apple, peeled, cored, and cut into tiny bits
¹/₄ cup walnuts, finely diced

This wild rice dish has a chewy texture with a nutty flavor.
The apple bits add a hint of sweetness.

Side Dishes

In a medium saucepan heat olive oil over medium-high heat.

Add celery, onion, and garlic. Reduce heat to low. Sauté until onions are tender and translucent.

Add wild rice and stir until combined. Then add hot vegetable broth and stir. Cover and simmer for 40 minutes.

Stir in apple bits and finely diced walnuts. Cover and simmer for an **additional** 20 minutes or until rice is tender and most of the liquid is absorbed.

Fluff with a fork and serve.

Makes 6 servings.

Side Dishes

Apple-Spiced Bulgar

2   Tbsp. extra-virgin olive oil
1   cup onion, chopped
1   clove garlic, minced
1   tsp. ground ginger
1   cup coarse bulgar wheat
1   can (14 oz.) vegetable broth
¼   tsp. ground cinnamon
1   medium sweet apple, peeled, cored, and finely diced
¼   cup golden raisins

This recipe can also be used as an entrée. Just double up on the portions and enjoy the health benefits which this vegetarian recipe has to offer: grain, fruits, and vegetables.

Side Dishes

In a large saucepan heat olive oil. Add onions, garlic, and ginger. Sauté until onions are soft, but not browned *(about 5 minutes)*.

Add bulgar wheat. Continue stirring until toasted *(about 3 minutes)*.

Stir in vegetable broth and cinnamon. Bring to a full boil.

Reduce heat to low. Cover and simmer for about 13 minutes or until bulgar is tender and liquid is absorbed.

Stir in finely diced apples and raisins.

Cover and cook for an **additional** two minutes.

Makes 6 to 8 servings.

Poultry

Poultry

Chicken Delicious

2 Tbsp. extra-virgin olive oil

1 medium onion, chopped

1 medium red pepper, chopped

3 small baking apples, peeled, cored, and sliced

¼ cup Port wine

¼ tsp. ground black pepper

⅛ tsp. salt

2 lbs. chicken breasts, boneless and skinless, cut in half and flattened

¼ cup bread crumbs

¼ cup Parmesan, finely shredded cheese

The combination of apples with red pepper gives this chicken dish a colorful presentation. Every bite is so moist with a unique taste that you don't even realize that fruit and vegetables were used in preparing this recipe.

Poultry

In a large skillet heat olive oil. Add onion and pepper.

Sauté until soft, but not browned.

Add apple slices, Port wine, black pepper, and salt. Cook over low heat, stirring occasionally with a wooden spoon, until apples are tender.

While the apple mixture is cooking prepare chicken:
Preheat oven to 400 degrees.

Butter an oven-proof glass dish large enough to contain the chicken breasts.

Coat both sides of the chicken pieces with bread crumbs. Place them in buttered dish.

Spoon cooked apple mixture over chicken.

Sprinkle finely shredded Parmesan cheese over the top.

Bake at 400 degrees for 30 minutes.

Serve over rice.

Makes 4 servings.

Poultry

Apple Walnut Chicken Salad

2 cups cooked chicken, cut into bite-size pieces
1 medium Granny Smith apple, peeled, cored, and finely chopped
1 cup celery, finely chopped
¹/₂ cup chopped walnuts
2 Tbsp. red onion, finely chopped
¹/₂ cup mayonnaise
¹/₈ tsp. ground black pepper

Whenever I make my heart-warming
chicken soup, I reserve the cooked chicken breast
to make this chicken salad.

Poultry

In a large bowl combine cooked chicken pieces, chopped apple, celery, walnuts, and onion.

Add mayonnaise and black pepper. Stir until combined.

For best flavor chill for at least 3 hours before serving.

Serve over a bed of lettuce or between two slices of bread.

Makes 4 to 6 servings.

Poultry

Apple Turkey Loaf

2   large eggs, beaten with a fork
1   medium apple, peeled, cored, and finely chopped
1   small onion, finely chopped
3/4   cup bread crumbs
2   Tbsp. catsup
1/2   tsp. parsley flakes
1/2   tsp. salt
1/4   tsp. ground black pepper
1/8   tsp. ground allspice
1/8   tsp. dry mustard
1   pkg. (1.3 lbs.) ground turkey (93% lean)

The chopped apples in this turkey loaf
give every bite a hint of sweetness.

Poultry

Preheat oven to 350 degrees.

In a large bowl combine all loaf ingredients **except** ground turkey. Mix well.

Crumble turkey over mixture. Mix thoroughly. (I use my hands.)

Spread in an ungreased 9- x 5- x 3-inch loaf pan.

Bake uncovered at 350 degrees for 45 to 50 minutes.

Remove from oven.

Allow loaf to rest for 10 minutes before slicing.

Makes 4 servings.

Seafood

Seafood

Baked Stuffed Shrimp

1 lb. jumbo tail-on shrimp, peeled and deveined

Stuffing

1	cup Panko bread crumbs
2	Tbsp. Parmesan, finely shredded cheese
½	cup (1 stick) butter, melted
1	Tbsp. lemon juice
1	Tbsp. cream sherry
1	garlic clove, minced
⅛	tsp. ground black pepper
1	medium Granny Smith apple, peeled, cored, and finely chopped
¼	cup pecans, finely chopped

*Expect this recipe to make 16 to 20 baked stuffed shrimp,
depending upon the size of the shrimp. Next time you're having
a gathering of family and friends, stuff the shrimp
earlier in the day and refrigerate them.
They'll be ready to bake once your guests arrive.
(Remember to preheat the oven.)*

Seafood

Preheat oven to 350 degrees.

Lightly grease a 13- x 9- x 2-inch glass oven-proof baking dish.

With tail upright, split the shrimp to "butterfly" them, forming a cavity to hold the stuffing. Set aside.

Stuffing

In a large bowl combine the bread crumbs and finely shredded Parmesan cheese.

Stir in the melted butter, lemon juice, sherry, minced garlic, and black pepper.

Add finely chopped apples and pecans. Stir until combined.

Using a tablespoon fill the cavity of each shrimp with the stuffing, curling the shrimp tail over the stuffing. Place each stuffed shrimp in the greased baking dish with the stuffing side up. (Distribute any remaining stuffing evenly amongst all the shrimp.)

Bake at 350 degrees for approximately 10 to 12 minutes or until shrimp turns a reddish-pink color.

Makes 4 servings.

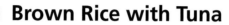

Seafood

Brown Rice with Tuna

- 2 Tbsp. extra-virgin olive oil
- 1 medium onion, chopped
- 1 medium Granny Smith apple, peeled, cored, and finely diced
- 1½ cups water
- ½ Tbsp. ground turmeric
- 2 cups Instant Brown Rice
- 1 can (12 oz.) chunk light tuna in water

Pressed for time and looking for a quick, nutritious meal?
This recipe is so simple and easy to make. Just add a garden salad
and some crusty bread. Voila! Dinner is served.

Seafood

In a large saucepan heat olive oil. Add chopped onion. Sauté until soft, but not browned *(about 3 to 5 minutes)*.

Add diced apples. Cook over medium-high heat, stirring occasionally with a wooden spoon, until apples are tender.

Add water and turmeric. Stir to combine. Then bring to a boil.

Stir in rice and tuna, including liquid. Reduce heat to low and cover pan.

Cook without stirring for 5 minutes.

Remove from stovetop. Let stand for 10 minutes.

Fluff with a fork before serving.

Makes 4 servings.

Seafood

Ed's Curried Tuna

- 2 Tbsp. extra-virgin olive oil
- 1 medium onion, chopped
- 4 small Granny Smith apples, peeled, cored, and coarsely chopped
- 1½ cups water
- 1 Tbsp. curry powder
- 2 cups Instant Brown Rice
- 2 cans (5 oz. each) chunk light tuna in water

For a nutritious and inexpensive meal consider making this curried tuna casserole. Not only is it simple to prepare but it only takes about 30 minutes from start to finish. To save time while the onions are sautéing, peel, core, and coarsely chop the apples.

Seafood

In a large saucepan heat olive oil. Add chopped onion. Sauté until soft, but not browned *(about 3 to 5 minutes)*.

Add chopped apples. Cook over medium heat, stirring occasionally with a wooden spoon, until apples are tender.

Add water and curry powder. Stir to combine. Then bring to a boil.

Stir in rice and tuna, including liquid, until well combined. Reduce heat to low and cover pan.

Cook without stirring for 5 minutes.

Remove from stovetop. Let stand for 5 minutes.

Fluff with a fork before serving.

Makes 4 to 6 servings.

Cakes & Brownies

Cakes & Brownies

Auntie's Apple Pudding Cake

7	or 8 medium apples, peeled, cored, and cut into chunks (Macs are good.)
¼	cup (¼ stick) Crisco®
½	cup sugar
1	large egg
1¼	cups all-purpose flour
1	tsp. baking powder
½	tsp. salt
½	cup milk
2	tsp. sugar
1	tsp. ground cinnamon

"I've had this recipe for 30 years. It was given to me by my favorite aunt who was always very special to me. Her apple pudding cake always warms my belly as thoughts of her warm my heart." – KATHLEEN SOUSA

Cakes & Brownies

In a medium saucepan slowly cook apple chunks until chunks become soft but still hold their shape.

While the apple chunks are cooking prepare cake batter:
In a large bowl cream Crisco® and sugar thoroughly. Add egg and beat well.

Combine together flour, baking powder, and salt.

Add dry ingredients to creamed mixture, alternately with milk, blending after each addition.

Preheat oven to 350 degrees.

Spray a 3-quart round casserole dish with cooking spray.

Arrange cooked apple chunks evenly on bottom of casserole dish.

Pour cake batter over the cooked apple chunks.

In a small dish combine sugar and cinnamon. Then sprinkle this mixture over the top of the cake batter.

Bake at 350 degrees for 45 minutes or until toothpick inserted in center comes out clean.

Makes approximately 8 servings

Cakes & Brownies

Dottie's Apple Cake

3 or 4 medium apples, peeled, cored, and sliced
3 Tbsp. sugar
$^3/_4$ tsp. ground cinnamon
3 cups all-purpose flour
2 cups sugar
1 Tbsp. baking powder
$^1/_4$ tsp. salt
1 cup vegetable oil
4 large eggs, beaten slightly
$^1/_4$ cup orange juice
1 Tbsp. vanilla extract

*"Everyone loves my cake with ice cream or whipped cream.
This old recipe has been passed around for many years.
I use whatever apples I have on hand when
making this cake."* – DOTTIE DUDLEY

Cakes & Brownies

Preheat oven to 325 degrees.

Generously butter a 9-inch tube pan.

In a small dish combine sugar and cinnamon. Set aside.

In a large bowl sift together flour, sugar, baking powder, and salt. Gradually stir in oil and slightly beaten eggs.

Add orange juice and vanilla extract. Beat until smooth.

Pour about half of the batter into the well-buttered tube pan. Arrange half of the apple slices on top of the batter. Lightly sprinkle the top with half of the sugar/cinnamon mixture.

Using a spatula add the remaining batter. Arrange the remaining apple slices and sprinkle the rest of the sugar/cinnamon mixture over the top.

Bake at 325 degrees for about 1 hour* and 30 minutes.

*Check the cake after one hour by inserting toothpick in center. Ready when pick comes out clean.

Makes 10 servings.

Cakes & Brownies

Spicy Applesauce Cake

- 1/2 cup (1 stick) butter, softened
- 1 cup sugar
- 1 tsp. ground cinnamon
- 1/2 tsp. ground cloves
- 1/4 tsp. ground nutmeg
- 1 tsp. baking soda
- 1 tsp. hot water
- 1 cup unsweetened applesauce
- 13/4 cups all-purpose flour
- 1 cup raisins
- Confectioners' sugar (to sprinkle over top after baking)

*Do you feel like having something spicy to go with
your hot cup of tea? This cake not only smells delicious as
it's baking but continues to permeate the air with its spices
as it sits on a plate waiting to be picked up and eaten.*

Cakes & Brownies

Preheat oven to 350 degrees.

Generously grease and flour a 13- x 9- x 2-inch baking pan.

In a large bowl, with mixer at low speed, cream butter, sugar, and spices until light and fluffy.

In a small bowl dissolve the baking soda in hot water.
Stir in unsweetened applesauce.

Add applesauce mixture to large bowl. Beat until well blended.

Add flour, stirring with a spoon until combined.

Fold in raisins.

Pour batter into greased and floured pan. Using a spatula spread batter evenly into the corners.

Bake at 350 degrees for 30 minutes or until toothpick inserted in center comes out clean.

Serve warm or cold with a generous sprinkle of confectioners' sugar.

Makes 12 servings.

Cakes & Brownies

Apple Fudge Cake

½	cup (1 stick) butter, melted
1½	cups dark-brown sugar
1	cup unsweetened applesauce
2	large eggs
2	tsp. vanilla extract
1¼	cups all-purpose flour
¼	cup unsweetened cocoa powder
1	tsp. baking powder
½	tsp. baking soda
½	cup apple, peeled, cored, and cut into tiny bites

A slice of this moist cake is as rich in flavor as a piece of fudge.
Be sure to use high quality unsweetened cocoa powder,
such as Ghirardelli, to attain the intense chocolate taste.

Cakes & Brownies

Preheat oven to 350 degrees.

Grease and flour an 8-inch square glass oven-proof baking dish.

In a large bowl, with mixer at high speed, beat melted butter, sugar, applesauce, eggs, and vanilla extract until well combined *(about one minute)*.

In a separate bowl sift together flour, cocoa powder, baking powder, and baking soda.

Add flour mixture to large bowl. Stir with a spoon until combined.

Fold in apple bites.

Pour batter into greased and floured baking dish. Using a spatula spread batter evenly into the corners.

Bake at 350 degrees for 35 minutes or until toothpick inserted in center comes out clean.

Cool completely on a wire rack before cutting.

Serve with whipped cream or vanilla ice cream.

Makes 8 servings.

Cakes & Brownies

Apple Nut Brownies

 2 large eggs
 1 cup sugar
 $\frac{1}{2}$ cup (1 stick) butter, melted
 $\frac{1}{2}$ cup unsweetened cocoa powder
 1 tsp. vanilla extract
 1 cup all-purpose flour
 $\frac{1}{4}$ tsp. baking powder
 $\frac{1}{8}$ tsp. salt
 1 medium apple, peeled, cored, and finely diced
 1 cup chopped walnuts

These brownies resemble fudge in many ways:
moist with an intense chocolate taste and loaded with nuts.
As mentioned in the previous recipe I use high quality
unsweetened cocoa powder, such as Ghirardelli.

Cakes & Brownies

Preheat oven to 350 degrees.

Grease a 9-inch square baking pan.

In a large bowl, with mixer at high speed, beat eggs well until foamy. Gradually add sugar, beating after each addition, until mixture is thick and light.

In a separate bowl combine melted butter and cocoa powder. Stir in vanilla extract.

Add chocolate mixture to large bowl. Beat on high until well combined *(about one minute)*.

Sift together flour, baking powder, and salt.

Add flour mixture to large bowl. Stir with a spoon until well combined.

Fold in diced apples and chopped walnuts. (Batter will be stiff.)

Pour batter into greased baking pan. Using a spatula spread batter evenly into the corners.

Bake at 350 degrees for about 30 minutes or until toothpick inserted in center comes out clean.

Cool completely on a wire rack before cutting into squares.

Makes 9 servings.

Buckle & Tortes

Buckle & Tortes

Apple Walnut Buckle

1 large egg
1/2 cup sugar
1 tsp. vanilla extract
1/3 cup all-purpose flour
1 tsp. baking powder
1/4 tsp. salt
2 large baking apples, peeled, cored, and diced
1/2 cup chopped walnuts
2 Tbsp. butter

*Buckles are cake-like desserts made with fresh fruit,
usually berries. Mine uses apples. The diced baking apples
used in this recipe make for a moist, sweet-tasting dessert that
resembles a buckle, especially with the apples peaking through the top.*

Buckle & Tortes

Preheat oven to 350 degrees.

Butter the bottom and sides of an 8-inch square glass oven-proof baking dish.

In a large bowl beat egg until foamy. Gradually add sugar, beating after each addition, until mixture is thick and light.

Beat in vanilla extract.

Add flour, baking powder, and salt. Stir until combined.

Fold in diced apples and chopped walnuts.

Pour batter into baking dish.

Dot with butter.

Bake at 350 degrees for 30 minutes until top is golden brown.

Transfer to cooling wire rack. Cool slightly.

Serve warm with whipped cream or vanilla ice cream.

Makes 6 servings.

Buckle & Tortes

Agnes's Apple Torte

½	cup (1 stick) butter, softened
1	cup sugar
2	large eggs
1¾	cups all-purpose flour, sifted
2	tsp. baking powder
½	tsp. salt
1	tsp. vanilla extract
8	large Granny Smith apples
🍎	Ground cinnamon (to sprinkle over top of apples)

Topping

½	cup (1 stick) butter, softened
1	cup sugar
2	large eggs

"This recipe is special to me because it was passed down by my mother-in-law, Agnes Munap. It is also special because it won first prize at my place of employment, H P Enterprise Services, in 'The Great Apple Cake Bake Off 2005.' There was no monetary prize, just the bragging right to say it was the best of all the homemade apple cake recipes.

"My mother-in-law, Agnes, is now 94 and still bakes all her favorite recipes." – JANICE BELASCO

Buckle & Tortes

Preheat oven to 350 degrees.

Grease and flour a 10-inch spring-form pan.

In a large bowl, with mixer at low speed, cream butter and sugar until smooth and fluffy. Add one egg at a time, making sure batter continues to be fluffy.

Add sifted flour, baking powder, salt, and vanilla extract. Blend thoroughly. (Mixture will be stiff.)

Spread mixture into greased and floured 10-inch spring-form pan.

Peel, pare, and core apples. Cut apples into length-wise slices and stand on end close together in the mixture until the entire mixture is covered with apples. Sprinkle top with cinnamon.

Bake at 350 degrees for about 1½ hours.

While torte is baking in the oven prepare topping:
Cream butter. Add sugar and eggs. Beat well.

Pour topping mixture over hot torte.

Bake an **additional** 15 minutes or until custard is set.

Makes 8 to 10 servings.

 *Buckle & Tortes*

Apple-Date Torte

$^3/_4$ cup sugar

$^1/_2$ cup all-purpose flour, sifted

2 tsp. baking powder

1 large egg

1 Tbsp. butter, melted

1 tsp. vanilla extract

4 medium baking apples, peeled, cored, and diced

$^1/_2$ cup chopped dates

$^1/_2$ cup chopped walnuts

The combination of apples, dates, and walnuts
not only gives this torte a crusty brown finish
but also tastes indescribably delicious.

Buckle & Tortes

Preheat oven to 400 degrees.

Generously grease a deep dish 9.5-inch glass pie plate with butter.

In a large bowl combine sugar, sifted flour, and baking powder.

Add egg, melted butter, and vanilla extract. Stir until thoroughly combined. Batter will be stiff.

Fold in diced apples, chopped dates, and chopped walnuts until apples, dates, and walnuts are completely coated with the batter.

Pour mixture into greased pie plate.

Bake (uncovered) at 400 degrees for the **first** 30 minutes.

Cover with aluminum foil and bake for an **additional** 10 to 15 minutes or until apples are tender.

Transfer to cooling wire rack. Cool slightly.

Serve warm with whipped cream.

Makes 8 servings.

Pies

Pies

Delicious Pecan Pie

- Pastry for a single-crust pie
- 4 medium Golden Delicious apples, peeled, cored, and sliced
- 2 large eggs
- 3/4 cup sugar
- 1/2 cup light corn syrup
- 1 Tbsp. butter, melted
- 1/2 tsp. vanilla extract
- 3/4 cup pecans, finely chopped

Golden Delicious apples reduce the amount of sugar needed and create an eye-appealing finished pie, comparable to those bought in gourmet pastry shops.

Pies

Preheat oven to 425 degrees.

Pastry-line a 10-inch glass pie plate.

Arrange apple slices evenly in pie plate.

In a medium-sized bowl beat eggs with a fork. Add sugar, corn syrup, melted butter, and vanilla extract. Mix with a spoon until well blended.

Stir in finely chopped pecans.

Slowly pour pecan mixture over apple slices, making sure to cover all apple slices with this mixture.

Bake at 425 degrees for the **first** 10 minutes.

Lower oven temperature to 300 degrees. Bake an **additional** 55 to 60 minutes or until knife inserted in center comes out clean.

Cool completely on a wire rack.

Serve with whipped cream.

Make 8 servings.

Pies

Apple Walnut Crispy Crust Pie

4   medium Granny Smith apples, peeled, cored, and sliced
1   Tbsp. sugar
1   tsp. ground cinnamon
¾   cup (1½ sticks) butter, melted
1   cup all-purpose flour
¾   cup sugar
1   large egg, beaten with a fork
½   cup chopped walnuts

*"It's worth doing a cookbook for just
this one recipe."* – EDWARD LODI

Pies

Preheat oven to 350 degrees.

Generously grease a deep dish 9.5-inch glass pie plate with butter.

Arrange apple slices evenly in greased pie plate.

In a small bowl combine sugar and cinnamon. Sprinkle this mixture to cover the apples.

In a large bowl combine melted butter, flour, sugar, and beaten egg. Mix with a spoon.

Fold in chopped walnuts.

Using a spatula carefully spread batter evenly over the apple slices and to the edge of the pie plate.

Bake at 350 degrees for 40 to 45 minutes or until golden brown.

Cool completely on a wire rack.

Serve with whipped cream or your favorite ice cream.

Makes 8 servings.

Pies

Old-Fashioned Apple Pie

- ☙ Pastry for a double-crust pie
- ³/₄ cup sugar
- 2 Tbsp. cornstarch
- 1 tsp. ground cinnamon
- ¹/₈ tsp. ground nutmeg
- 7 medium baking apples, peeled, cored, and thinly sliced
- 1 Tbsp. butter

*When I was a child my father would sit at the kitchen table
peeling apples from his own trees while my mother
made the pie crust from scratch.*

*Making this pie today from our own espaliered Beverly Hills apple tree
brought back those fond memories. When Ed and I bought the tree
fifteen years ago I hardly dared hope that it would produce apples
for a scrumptious apple pie.*

Pies

Preheat oven to 425 degrees.

Pastry-line a 9-inch glass pie plate.

In a large bowl combine sugar, cornstarch, cinnamon, and nutmeg.

Add apple slices. Toss gently until apples are well coated.

Pour mixture into the lined pie plate.

Dot with butter.

Place top crust over apple filling. Seal and flute the edge. Cut slits in the top crust.

Bake at 425 degrees for about 35 to 40 minutes (cover edge of crust with strips of foil after the first 10 to 15 minutes of baking) or until apples are tender and top is golden. Juice from the apples will start to bubble over the crust.

Cool completely on a wire rack.

Makes 8 servings.

Crisps

Crisps

My Pen Pal's Apple Crisp

10 to 12 medium apples, peeled, cored, and sliced
 1 cup all-purpose flour
 1 cup sugar
 1 tsp. baking powder
 1 large egg
 1/4 tsp. salt
 3/4 cup (1 1/2 sticks) butter, melted

Topping

 3/4 cup sugar
 1 heaping tsp. ground cinnamon

ↀↀↀ

"This apple crisp is the best I've ever had thanks to a pen pal who always exchanges recipes with me." – MAUREEN DION

Crisps

Preheat oven to 350 degrees.

Grease a 13- x 9- x 2-inch baking pan.

Place apple slices in the greased baking pan. Set aside.

In a large bowl combine flour, sugar, baking powder, egg, and salt until crumbly.

Sprinkle crumbly mixture over the sliced apples. Then pour melted butter over the top.

Topping

Measure sugar in a large measuring cup. Add heaping teaspoon of cinnamon. Mix well with a spoon.

Evenly sprinkle sugar/cinnamon mixture over the top.

Bake at 350 degrees for 45 minutes.

Makes 12 servings.

Apple Oatmeal Crisp

6 cups baking apples, peeled, cored, and chopped

½ cup rolled oats

½ cup all-purpose flour

½ cup dark-brown sugar

1 tsp. ground cinnamon

¼ tsp. ground allspice

⅓ cup *cold* butter, cut into small pieces

*Last fall my good friend Carolyn Gilmore surprised me
with a bag containing several varieties of local apples,
some perfect for eating, others with marks and bruises that
needed to be used up soon. What better way than in a crisp?*

Crisps

Preheat oven to 375 degrees.

Butter the bottom and sides of an 8-inch square glass oven-proof baking dish.

Pour chopped apples into baking dish. Set aside.

In a large bowl whisk oats, flour, sugar, cinnamon, and allspice. Using a pastry cutter, cut in butter until mixture forms crumbs.

Sprinkle crumbly mixture over top of chopped apples. Cover dish with aluminum foil.

Bake at 375 degrees for 25 minutes. Remove aluminum foil and cook for an **additional** 10 to 15 minutes or until top is golden brown and juice from the apples bubbles up from the bottom of the dish.

Transfer to cooling wire rack. Cool slightly.

Serve warm with whipped cream or your favorite ice cream.

Makes 6 servings.

Crisps

Granny's Apple Crisp

- ½ cup sugar
- 1 tsp. ground cinnamon
- 5 large Granny Smith apples, peeled, cored, and coarsely chopped
- 1 cup cranberries, fresh or frozen, whole

Topping

- 6 Tbsp. (¾ stick) butter, softened
- ¾ cup rolled oats
- ¾ cup all-purpose flour
- ½ cup sugar

The aroma of this crisp cooking in the oven evokes, for me, childhood dreams of a Granny I never knew. I hope it evokes fond memories for you, too.

In the early 1950's my parents left their family and friends in Pico, one of the Azorean islands, and immigrated to the United States. A couple of years later I was born. Throughout my childhood I wondered what my grandparents were like. The years have passed but my childhood dreams of Granny live in Granny's Apple Crisp.

Crisps

Preheat oven to 350 degrees.

Butter the bottom and sides of a 2-quart oblong (2-inch deep) glass oven-proof baking dish.

In a large bowl combine sugar and cinnamon.

Add chopped apples and cranberries. Toss gently until fruits are well coated.

Pour mixture into baking dish.

Topping

In a medium-sized bowl stir all topping ingredients with a fork until crumbly.

Sprinkle over top of fruits.

Bake at 350 degrees for 1 hour.

Transfer to cooling wire rack. Cool slightly.

Serve warm with whipped cream or your favorite ice cream.

Makes 8 servings.

Crisps

Apple Berry Crisp

4 cups baking apples, peeled, cored, and chopped

1 cup blueberries, fresh or frozen

1 cup cranberries, fresh or frozen, cut in half

1/2 cup rolled oats

1/2 cup all-purpose flour

1/2 cup sugar

1 tsp. ground cinnamon

1/4 cup (1/2 stick) *cold* butter, cut into small pieces

*Every year I not only freeze fresh blueberries that my husband
and I pick locally during the summer, but I also freeze fresh cranberries
that I buy at the annual Cranberry Harvest Celebration in Wareham,
Massachusetts. Because of my love for these berries I developed this
apple crisp. I hope that you will enjoy it as much as we do.*

Crisps

Preheat oven to 375 degrees.

Butter the bottom and sides of an 8-inch square glass oven-proof baking dish.

Pour chopped apples into baking dish.

Sprinkle blueberries over the apples followed by the halved cranberries. Set aside.

In a large bowl whisk oats, flour, sugar, and cinnamon. Using a pastry cutter, cut in butter until mixture forms crumbs.

Sprinkle crumbly mixture over top of berries. Cover dish with aluminum foil.

Bake at 375 degrees for 45 minutes. Remove aluminum foil and cook for an **additional** 20 to 25 minutes or until top is golden brown and juice from the fruits bubbles through.

Transfer to cooling wire rack. Cool slightly.

Serve warm with whipped cream or your favorite ice cream.

Makes 6 servings.

Crisps

Blueberry Apple Crisp

4 medium baking apples, peeled, cored, and chopped
2 cups blueberries, fresh or frozen
³/₄ cup rolled oats
¹/₃ cup all-purpose flour
¹/₃ cup dark-brown sugar, firmly packed
1 tsp. ground cinnamon
¹/₄ cup (¹/₂ stick) *cold* butter, cut into small pieces

*As I started out to make my Apple Berry Crisp (see previous recipe),
I discovered that I didn't have enough chopped apples on hand. I solved
the problem by adding blueberries. With more rolled oats and less sugar,
this crisp is sure to please those looking for a nutritious dessert.*

Crisps

Preheat oven to 375 degrees.

Butter the bottom and sides of an 8-inch square glass oven-proof baking dish.

Pour chopped apples into baking dish.

Sprinkle blueberries over the apples. Set aside.

In a large bowl whisk oats, flour, sugar, and cinnamon. Using a pastry cutter, cut in butter until mixture forms crumbs.

Sprinkle crumbly mixture over top of berries. Cover dish with aluminum foil.

Bake at 375 degrees for 45 minutes. Remove aluminum foil and cook for an **additional** 20 to 25 minutes or until top is golden brown and juice from the fruits bubbles through.

Transfer to cooling wire rack. Cool slightly.

Serve warm with whipped cream or your favorite ice cream.

Makes 6 servings.

Crisps

Apple Cranberry Crisp

Apple/Cranberry Mixture

- 4 medium baking apples, peeled, cored, and chopped
- 2½ cups fresh or frozen cranberries
- ¾ cup granulated sugar

Topping

- ½ cup (1 stick) butter, melted
- 1½ cups rolled oats
- ½ cup dark-brown sugar
- ⅓ cup all-purpose flour
- ¼ cup chopped walnuts

My love for cranberries is such that I've chosen to complete this section with the following crisp. The combination of cranberries and apples gives every bite a unique taste, sweet with a hint of tartness.

Crisps

Preheat oven to 350 degrees.

Butter the bottom and sides of a 13- x 9- x 2-inch glass oven-proof baking dish.

Apple/Cranberry Mixture

In a large bowl combine apples, cranberries, and sugar. Toss until fruits are covered with sugar. Spread evenly over bottom of baking dish. Set aside.

Topping

In a medium-sized bowl stir topping ingredients until combined. Sprinkle evenly over fruits.

Bake at 350 degrees for 35 to 40 minutes or until fruit is soft and juice from the fruits bubbles.

Transfer to cooling wire rack. Cool slightly.

Serve warm.

Makes 12 servings.

About the Author

Yolanda Lodi loves to create nutritious and easy to prepare dishes to satisfy her own tastes and to share with family and friends. She is the author of four previous cookbooks: *Yolanda's Cranberry Country Recipes*, an eclectic collection of traditional and original recipes; *Yolanda's Hand-Me-Down Recipes*, an assortment of recipes rich in New England's cultural heritage; *Yolanda's Blueberry Cookbook*, her most popular cookbook, not only in Massachusetts but also in Maine; and *Yolanda's All New Cranberry Cookbook*, with recipes that use not only fresh and frozen cranberries but sweetened dried cranberries as well. Compiling these collections brought so much enjoyment to her that she decided to compile an *All Apple Cookbook*. Besides recipes and stories, these cookbooks feature an introduction in which she offers encouragement for those who love to cook and want to be creative in developing their own recipes. "Take chances in experimenting with different ingredients," she urges her readers. "Try something new that sounds good. Start with fresh ingredients that you're familiar with and then experiment."

Yolanda looks forward to discussing the process of compiling and preserving recipes with those she meets while promoting her cookbooks. She hopes that these cookbooks will inspire others to gather and preserve their own special recipes; she strongly feels that preserving recipes keeps traditions alive for future generations to cherish. Yolanda is also co-editor of the recent, highly acclaimed anthology, *Cranberry Memories: Voices from the Bogs*.

She grew up in Fairhaven and lives in a log house in Middleborough with her husband, Edward, her greatest fan and taste tester. When not exhibiting at shows and fairs, she's at home gardening, reading, or cooking – an activity she's enjoyed since her teens.

Notes

Notes

Notes